STRAIGHT JACKET WINTER

STRAIGHT JACKET WINTER

ESTHER DUQUETTE & **GILLES POULIN-DENIS**

PLAYWRIGHTS CANADA PRESS
TORONTO

LIBRARY AND ARCHIVES CANADA CATALOGUING IN PUBLICATION
Title: Straight jacket winter / Esther Duquette, Gilles Poulin-Denis.
Names: Duquette, Esther, author. | Poulin-Denis, Gilles, 1980- author.
Description: First edition.
Identifiers: Canadiana 20190191791 | ISBN 9780369100559 (softcover)
Classification: LCC PS8607.U696 S77 2019 | DDC C812/.6—dc23

Playwrights Canada Press acknowledges that we operate on land, which, for thousands of years, has been the traditional territories of the Mississaugas of the Credit, Huron-Wendat, Anishinaabe, Métis, and Haudenosaunee peoples. Today, this meeting place is home to many Indigenous peoples from across Turtle Island and we are grateful to have the opportunity to work and play here.

We acknowledge the financial support of the Canada Council for the Arts—which last year invested $153 million to bring the arts to Canadians throughout the country—the Ontario Arts Council (OAC), Ontario Creates, and the Government of Canada for our publishing activities.

Canada Council for the Arts
Conseil des arts du Canada

ONTARIO ARTS COUNCIL
CONSEIL DES ARTS DE L'ONTARIO
an Ontario government agency
un organisme du gouvernement de l'Ontario

Canada

ONTARIO CREATES | ONTARIO CRÉATIF

À Réjean Ducharme et Claire Richard. Merci.

To all the Andrés and Nicoles of the world, may
you find your place, your home in this life.

Straight Jacket Winter was first produced by 2PAR4, the National Art Centre's French Theatre, and Théâtre la Seizième at Théâtre Periscope in Québec City on May 27, 2016, as part of Carrefour international de théâtre de Québec. It featured the following cast and creative team:

Esther: Esther Duquette
Gilles: Gilles Poulin-Denis
Man: Frédéric Lemay
Woman: Julie Trépanier

Directors: Esther Duquette and Gilles Poulin-Denis
Assistant Director: Édith Patenaude
Set Design: Julie Vallée-Léger
Costume Design: Drew Facey
Lighting Design: Itai Erdal
Sound Design: Antoine Berthiaume and Jacques Poulin-Denis
Video Design: Antoine Quirion-Couture
Dramaturg: Philippe Ducros
Artistic Advisor: Craig Holzschuh
Stage Manager and Technical Director: Julien Veronneau and Kitty Hoffman
Touring Stage Manager: Dominique Cuerrier
Touring Technical Director: Clémence Doray

NOTE TO THE READER

The play is written for four performers: both playwrights plus two actors, but it can also be performed by four actors.

The stage is divided into two spaces:

1. In the centre of the stage is a raised platform. This space will serve as the different apartments throughout the piece and will be used by the actors.

2. The rest of the stage—the space around the platform— will be used by the playwrights. All the items used in the various apartments are stored stage left, with two tables placed stage right.

In order to simplify reading the script, it has been divided in two. The left-hand column shows the playwrights' dialogue and actions, and the right-hand one shows that of the actors.

CHARACTERS

Esther
Gilles
Woman
Man

Note: Esther and the Woman and Gilles and the Man are the
same characters but at two different times. Esther and Gilles
are in the present, engaging the audience directly, while the
Woman and the Man are in the past, re-enacting scenes of
Esther and Gilles's life/story.

PROLOGUE
RUE DORION, MONTRÉAL

HAPPY NEW YEAR

December 31, 2010
Rue Dorion, Montréal

As the audience enters the theatre, the MAN and WOMAN greet them, wishing them a happy new year. They have party hats on.

During this time, GILLES and ESTHER are selecting records and playing them on the turntable. They prepare their props for the show.

Once the audience is seated, the MAN and WOMAN make their way to the centre of the stage.

MAN: *(to audience)* Thank you all for coming tonight. It's so good to see your faces before our big move. We are gonna miss you all and we would just like to say . . .

WOMAN: Hurry, it's almost time.

MAN: What?

WOMAN: It's almost midnight.

MAN: Oh! Okay, it's almost midnight. Are you ready for the countdown?

AUDIENCE: YES!

GILLES pulls out his smartphone and starts recording.

ALL: Ten, nine, eight, seven, six, five, four, three, two, one . . .

Happy New Year!

MAN and WOMAN kiss.

ESTHER plays a song on the record player. It's "Ce n'est qu'un au revoir"—the French version of "Auld Lang Syne." She and GILLES signal to the audience to sing along.

AUDIENCE: *(singing)*
Ce n'est qu'un au revoir, mes frères
Ce n'est qu'un au revoir
Oui, nous nous reverrons, mes frères
Ce n'est qu'un au revoir

This is not goodbye, my friends
This is not goodbye
We'll surely see each
other again
This is not goodbye

For auld lang syne, my dear
For auld lang syne
We'll take a cup of kindness yet
For auld lang syne

The MAN and WOMAN hold each other close, truly moved by the song.

WOMAN: Merci.

MAN: Thank you.

GILLES turns to ESTHER and smiles. He exits the stage and returns to the turntable.

The MAN turns to the WOMAN and smiles, knowing they won't see each other for a long time. He exits the stage. She watches him leave, heavy-hearted.

PART 1

BUTE STREET, VANCOUVER

VERTIGO

It's snowing.

*ESTHER brings the WOMAN a
bag and helps her slip on
a coat.*

*The WOMAN grabs her bag and
turns to face the emptiness in
front of her, the unknown of her
new life.*

ESTHER: A couple of winters
ago, there was a huge snow-
storm. The next day, I drove
out of town. The road was
covered with immaculate
white snow and the sky was
cloudy and gray. I couldn't
see the sun, just a blinding
white light coming through
the clouds. I remember at
one point I couldn't see
any trees, or hydro poles,
or houses. The horizon had
completely disappeared. I

felt lost in all that whiteness,
a small dot on a white page.

January 28, 2011
Bute Street, Vancouver

*The WOMAN takes a deep breath
and walks into her very small
and bare sublet. She looks
around her new place and
suddenly feels very far away
from home.*

*The WOMAN pulls out a few
books from her bag, as well as
a computer and a phone. She
tries to organize these items on
the floor. She leaves and returns
with a small stool.*

*She picks up her phone, dials
a number, and puts it on
speakerphone.*

TELEPHONE: Thank you for
choosing Shaw. For service in
English, please press one.

选择国语服务，请按「二」。

選擇廣東話，請按「三」。

ਪੰਜਾਬੀ ਵਿਚ ਸੇਵਾ ਲਈ, ਚਾਰ ਦਬਾਉ।

*She waits for the French option
in the menu, but it never comes.*

Please choose an option
from the following menu.
For service in English, please
press one.

选择国语服务，请按「二」。

選擇廣東話，請按「三」。

ਪੰਜਾਬੀ ਵਿਚ ਸੇਵਾ ਲਈ, ਚਾਰ ਦਬਾਓ।

She hits number one.

For technical support, press
one. For new and additional
services, equipment activation,
or to schedule an appointment,
press two. For billing inquiries
and . . .

*She hits another number. The
phone rings.*

Thank you for choosing Shaw.
This is Derek, how can I assist
you today?

*The WOMAN quickly picks up her
phone and turns off the speaker.*

WOMAN: Yes, hi. I euh ... I need dee Internet ...
Oh. Esther Duquette ...
(slowly) Esther Duquette ...
Uhm, Es-Teux. Ducouette?
D-U-Q-U-E-T-T-E ...
Yes ... 925 Boote Street in Vancouver.
Boote street ...
In de West Hend?
Ah, Bute Street.
Okay. How long before dey come? Sorry?
Two weeks?! Oh ...
Is it possible to ave it more fast? ...
No, it's because I just move two day ago and ...
Okay. No, I understand.
Tank you.

She hangs up, disappointed by the delay.

FRESH START

ESTHER: We moved to Vancouver because I got a new job. I had been looking for work in Montréal but wasn't really finding anything. Gilles sent me a job offer from a Vancouver theatre company. He had worked for them before and they were looking for a director of communications. It was perfect for me, plus Gilles had always wanted to go back to Vancouver.

We were so excited to discover the West Coast. The mountains, the beaches, the snowless winters. At the time, it felt like we were going on vacation. A two-year-long vacation, the length of my contract.

We rented our Montréal condo to a couple from

France. We left them all of
our belongings: our furniture, our sheets, our dishes,
even our plants.

We left everything except a
few items that we packed in
seven small boxes. We then
shipped them to Vancouver
by bus.

*GILLES hands boxes to the
WOMAN.*

*The WOMAN lines up the seven
boxes in her very small sublet.*

I had to wait two whole
weeks for those boxes.

We packed a computer, a few
pairs of shoes, an English
dictionary, a printer, but
also weird things like books
we'd already read, a cushion, and . . . a cheese grater.
I guess the cheese practices
outside of Quebec were
unclear to me.

We also brought a dozen
records. We'd look at the
covers and imagine the

music . . . because we left the turntable back in Montréal.

The WOMAN opens up a few boxes, looking for something.

She pulls out a few books. One of them is Réjean Ducharme's L'hiver de force. *She reads a few pages.*

ESTHER: *(reading a postcard)*
Geneviève Duquette
36, chemin Duquette
Fulford, Québec, Canada

My Dear Sister,

I'm slowly discovering my new city. The image on the front is of the Burrard Bridge. I cross it every day to get to work. I love my new job here, plus I have a great view of the mountains from my office.

It's odd being in a city where no one knows you. I feel free to reinvent myself.

I hope all is well at the farm.
I would've liked to have been
with you all for Mom's birth-
day. Thanks for organizing it.

I miss you a lot.

Esther

SKYPE

A Skype call interrupts the WOMAN's reading. She answers. Her face lights up as the MAN's face appears on the screen.

WOMAN: Hi!

MAN: Hey, love. How's it going?

WOMAN: Good. You? Where are you?

MAN: I'm still at the theatre. I have to be on stage soon, but I wanted to call and see if everything was okay.

WOMAN: Do you want to talk later?

MAN: No, I still have time. So, how was it picking up those boxes?

WOMAN: Not too bad. The taxi driver helped me bring them in.

MAN: Good. I wish I was there to help you with that.

WOMAN: I know . . . It was fine.

MAN: So, what else did you do today?

WOMAN: I walked around town, on the seawall. It's amazing. I took a bunch of pictures. Oh, and I started reading *L'hiver de force* again.

MAN: We brought that book with us?

WOMAN: Yeah, it was in one of the boxes. I didn't remember the main characters being so weird.

MAN: What do you mean?

WOMAN: Well, they shut themselves in, then get rid of all their things. Remember? They throw their records out the window.

MAN: Oh yeah.

WOMAN: Yeah. It's really well written.

MAN: Hmm, I'll have to read it again. I hope you're not too bored out there.

WOMAN: No . . . I just can't wait for you to get here. You're going to love the neighbourhood. We're right next to Stanley Park. We'll go once you're here.

MAN: Can't wait.

GILLES: *(to the MAN)* Hey, we're gonna need you on stage soon.

(to GILLES) Oh, okay: coming.

(to the WOMAN) Sorry. I have to go, I'm in the next scene. Talk soon?

WOMAN: Okay. When?

MAN: Thursday night?

WOMAN: Okay.

MAN: Love you.

WOMAN: Love you too. Bye.

The WOMAN stares blankly at the now empty screen. As she closes the laptop, the apartment falls dark.

BO-BEC

The WOMAN tidies up the apartment.

ESTHER: I met Gilles on a warm Montréal summer night in 2006.

I had spent the day with my friend Virginie. After dinner, she wanted to meet up with this guy Jacques at an ice cream shop. I didn't feel like going but I went anyway.

When we got to Bo-Bec Ice Cream on Laurier Avenue, Jacques was there, but so was his brother Gilles. I know that meeting the love of your life in front of an ice cream shop is a little old school, but that's how it happened.

GILLES puts on a record: At Last! *by Etta James.*

He smiled at me, we started
talking and never stopped
till late into the night. At
two a.m. I ran away like
Cinderella to catch the last
bus: he ran after me and
asked for my number as the
bus doors were closing.

*GILLES helps the MAN put on a
dress shirt.*

                  The WOMAN unties her hair.

May 7, 2011

                  *The MAN walks into the
apartment.*

*ESTHER lights some sparklers.
Fireworks.*

                  *The MAN and WOMAN look into
each other's eyes. They hug
slowly and awkwardly and slow
dance to the music.*

*GILLES enters with a smoke
machine and surrounds them
with a cloud of pink smoke.*

                  They murmur a few sentences.

Music fades.

Finally, the MAN looks around at the apartment.

MAN: Right ... It's a bit small.

WOMAN: Yep.

They look around one more time ... and decide to move out.

PART 2
OAK STREET, VANCOUVER

MOVING

June 1, 2011
Oak Street, Vancouver

The MAN and WOMAN carry a couch and a table into their new, slightly bigger apartment. They sit on the couch, happy with their new place.

GILLES: I grew up in Saskatoon. There, when you reach the city limits, you won't find any suburbs, just endless fields.

When I was kid, I could never fall asleep in the car. I remember driving back from my grandparents' farm, I could see the city lights in the distance. They were so far away, it felt like we were speeding towards them but never getting any closer. And there was always a moment when I thought we would never be able to get back home.

WELCOME BC

The WOMAN is doing some research on her laptop.

MAN: What are you doing?

WOMAN: Looking for English classes.

MAN: Find anything?

WOMAN: Yeah, there's something great on this BC website.

ESTHER: On welcomebc.ca, which is only in English, it says:

GILLES: After English, the most common languages spoken in BC are Cantonese and Mandarin, Punjabi, German, Tagalog, French, Korean, Spanish, and Farsi.

Canada has two official languages: English and French.

People who immigrate to British Columbia do not need to understand French. However, you should be able to speak, read, and write in English.

WOMAN: They offer free courses.

They read a bit more of the website.

MAN: It's only for immigrants.

WOMAN: But I am an immigrant.

MAN: But you're not from another country.

WOMAN: Okay. So if I was from the States or Australia I would be eligible for English classes?

MAN: Exactly.

WOMAN: That makes sense. Because I feel right at home here, even though I can't communicate with people.

MAN: Your English is fine.

WOMAN: It's terrible.

MAN: What?

She understands that he's trying to make her speak in English. She plays along.

WOMAN: My Hinglish is bad.

The MAN smiles, trying not to laugh.

MAN: Your Hinglish is bad?

WOMAN: YES! Yesterday I ad to myma-am.

MAN: What?

WOMAN: I said: I ad to MYMA-AM!

MAN: . . .

WOMAN: I had to mime a ham. The butcher at the grocery store couldn't understand my accent.

MAN: You mimed a ham?

WOMAN: Yes.

MAN: Show me.

WOMAN: My ham mime?

MAN: Yes, your ham mime.

WOMAN: No.

MAN: Come on!

She smiles, and then proceeds to mime a ham. The MAN laughs.

Amazing.

WOMAN: So what do I do now, get private classes?

MAN: I'll help you.

WOMAN: You'll teach me English?

MAN: No, but we can practise together. Look.

He grabs the English dictionary and looks for a word.

Okay . . . I'll read the definition and you guess the word. "Something or someone absent, not found, or lost."

WOMAN: Not there? . . .
Uhm . . . Missing!

MAN: Good. Okay,
another one.

He finds another word.

This one's harder. "An area
of land, usually in a largely
natural state, reserved for the
enjoyment of the public."

WOMAN: Easy. A park.

MAN: See, tu es already more
bilingue.

WOMAN: Thank you beaucoup.

She prepares to leave for work.

What are you doing today?

MAN: I think I'll write. What
time are you back?

WOMAN: Around six.

MAN: Okay.

She goes for the door. Without looking back:

WOMAN: Bye, love.

MAN: Bye.

She exits.

WORK DAY

The MAN looks around him: the apartment is still pretty bare. He opens a box and takes out a few books, the cheese grater, and the Réjean Ducharme book. He goes to the computer and gets to work.

GILLES looks at the MAN for a moment, then turns to the audience.

GILLES: I'm self-employed, so I can work pretty much anywhere. I'm actually away more often than I'm home. I work in Montréal, Québec City, Ottawa, Winnipeg, but also exotic places like Brussels, Paris, Barcelona... Sudbury.

When I first arrived in Vancouver, I'd just finished a contract in Saskatoon where I spent all my days with

three really close friends.
And literally overnight, there
I was, all alone in front of my
computer.

*The MAN types on his computer.
He reads back what he just
wrote.*

MAN: "Despite the fact that
Réjean Ducharme is a literary
icon in Québec, he remains
relatively unknown to the
Canadian public. The social
alienation suffered by the pro-
tagonists is still a very current
subject despite the fact that
the novel *L'hiver de force* was
written in 1973."

*He erases the last few sen-
tences. He stops and thinks for
a moment. He picks up the novel
and paces around the room.*

At the time, I was applying
for a grant from the Canada
Council for the Arts to
translate Réjean Ducharme's
novel to English.

For those not familiar with
L'hiver de force, it is set in

1970s Montréal. The two main characters, André and Nicole, feel rejected by society and decide to live a marginal life.

It's important to note that André and Nicole are siblings, but their relationship is a bit ambiguous. They work together, they live together, they sleep in the same bed . . . they literally spend all of their time together.

The MAN sets down the novel. He picks up his cellphone and dials.

Hi, it's me . . .
So, what are you up to? . . .
Oh okay . . .
Well, I'm working on my grant application and I'm stumped . . .
I don't know how to translate the title.
You know, *L'hiver de force*? . . .
How would you translate that?
No, I know. But if I say *L'hiver de force*, what image comes to mind? . . .

Yeah, but it's a translation
grant. I should at least be able
to translate the title.
Okay, okay . . .
Hey, have you had lunch? . . .
What did you eat? . . . Really?
No, I just thought we could
have lunch together . . .
It's fine, I'll make myself some
eggs or something.
Okay, I'll let you get back
to work. What time are you
home? . . .
At six, right. I forgot. Okay, see
you then . . .

*The MAN goes back to his com-
puter. He types a few words,
but his heart isn't in it. He flops
onto the couch and starts playing a game on his phone.*

BEACHED

Lights go out. Total darkness.

ESTHER: One summer night, we decided to go watch the meteor showers. We went to the darkest place we could find in the city, a beach near the university.

When we got there, we noticed the sky was completely overcast. We couldn't see the stars. We couldn't see anything, not even the tips of our noses.

Still, we decided to sit on the beach and eat our picnic in the dark. We could see the city lights shining across the bay. It was a Friday night, and we tried imagining what people were doing behind the glimmering windows.

That's when we heard something splashing in the water
right in front of us. It was so
close we could've touched it.

I pointed my flashlight at
the sound. It was a little
sea otter, eating shells on
the shore. It didn't even
notice us. Normally an
animal should've sensed our
presence ...

We felt invisible.

THE FRIEND

The MAN and WOMAN are in the apartment. The MAN is setting up a table.

GILLES: In the following months, we tried different ways to meet people. Esther took dance classes, design classes, yoga classes. I did some unpaid work on a couple projects. We took up memberships to a few theatres hoping to meet people. And ... it almost worked.

WOMAN: What time is it?

The MAN pulls out his cellphone.

MAN: Ten o'clock.

WOMAN: I don't think she's gonna call.

MAN: Why do you say that?

WOMAN: It's late.

MAN: Not that late.

Pause.

WOMAN: Why don't we call her?

MAN: No, she said she'd let us know after dinner. We just need to wait.

WOMAN: Yeah, you're right.

Pause.

Give me your phone.

MAN: Why?

WOMAN: I'm going to text her to see if she's planning to call us.

MAN: Is that allowed?

WOMAN: I don't know. But if we're going to go out for a drink, I'd like to know.

MAN: Okay.

He hands her his phone. The WOMAN writes a text message. The MAN looks over her shoulder. As soon as she's done, he takes the phone and rereads the message. He nods approvingly and goes back to his task. The phone dings. He grabs his phone.

WOMAN: What does she say?

MAN: She says she doesn't plan on calling us and she doesn't plan on not calling us.

WOMAN: *(sadly)* That's kind of rude.

MAN: You shouldn't have texted her. She probably thinks we're desperate.

WOMAN: Well, she's the one who kept saying the other night that she loved us and she wanted to see us again.

MAN: I know. I don't get it. People try to be so likeable and when we like them, they're not happy.

WOMAN: Tell her we'll meet her anywhere.

The MAN hesitates.

MAN: Nah, I'll tell her we just really feel like meeting up for a drink. You know, chill.

He sends a text message. Pause.

Oh! She's writing back!

The WOMAN scurries over to the MAN and they look at the phone anxiously.

The phone dings.

She says she's on a date. If she calls us it'll be before eleven.

WOMAN: What time is it now?

MAN: 10:15.

The MAN and the WOMAN sit down on the couch. They both stare at the phone intensely.

GILLES holds a copy of Réjean Ducharme's L'Hiver de force.

GILLES: Page 147: "Everyone has to hold back from giving themselves completely. People want the least of you possible."

10:55 p.m.

"The least possible amount of words in a sentence, the least sentences in a letter, the least letters in a year ... "

11:05 p.m.

FALSE FRIENDS

GILLES: We never had problems making friends before—in general, we find ourselves fairly likeable—so we didn't understand why suddenly we were having such a hard time making friends.

ESTHER: Jeremy. I met him in my graphic design class. We worked together on a couple of assignments. At the end of the semester, I suggested we keep in touch. He said it was a good idea, but I sensed that he was just being polite.

GILLES: Caitlin Howden. We met her at an improv show. She's from Montréal and was also having a hard time making friends. So we decided to be friends that night at the bar. She invited us to make bread with her the next day, but she never texted us her address. If anyone here knows Caitlin, we're still up for some bread making.

ESTHER: Julie Duret. Julie was my colleague. We became friends, but not long afterwards she decided to move back to France. That happens often in Vancouver. It happened with Julie, but also with Cory, Siona and Alex, Craig, Claire, Angèle and Matt, Hugues and Sophie, and Julie Trépanier . . . It seems as though as soon as we get close to someone, they end up moving away.

GILLES: Blake William Turner. I met Blake on a show in Edmonton a few years back. He also lives in Vancouver. Whenever I run into him on the street, we always say we should hang out more, but we never follow up on it.

ESTHER: Blaine and Eliza. We saw them a few times.

They really wanted to be friends with us . . . and we found that a bit weird. So we stopped seeing them.

GILLES: Mark and Anita. We're very proud of this friendship. Only, Mark is always on tour and both Anita and I often work out of town. So the four of us are rarely in the city at the same time. We see each other on average about . . . twelve hours a year. A while ago, they sent us this.

GILLES plays MARK and ANITA's video.

ANITA: Hey guys.

MARK: I hope you're having a good time wherever you are—Vancouver, I think.

ANITA: Vancouver, yeah.

MARK: Uhm, we don't know where we are.

ANITA: Somewhere in Europe.

MARK: Yeah, somewhere in Europe. So we thought we would send kind of an SOS slash how are you?

ANITA: Sorry, we wanted to make a good video for you but ...

MARK: Yeah, we don't really know how. Anyway /

ANITA: Anyway.

MARK: / we got to get back to figuring out where the fuck we are.

ANITA: Yeah. We love you guys.

MARK: Bye.

ANITA: Au revoir.

The camera pans, revealing the Eiffel Tower.

MARK: Should we go this way?

ANITA: I don't know. I think it's maybe over there.

ANOTHER MIDSUMMER

*The MAN and WOMAN walk into
the apartment. They take their
jackets off in silence.*

MAN: What a crappy show.

WOMAN: Yeah, it wasn't
very good.

MAN: It was so bad. Why
would you put on another
Midsummer Night's Dream?
And to do it like that! I mean,
they had period costumes
and . . . wigs!

Pause.

Admit it. It was bad.

WOMAN: Yeah . . .

MAN: It's a comedy. They were
acting like it was Greek trag-
edy . . . I mean if you're going
to put it up, update it, or say

49

something with it, don't just do another fucking Shakespeare. It's like everyone's always producing Shakespeare in this town. I can't believe people stood up at the end. It's like we didn't see the same show.

WOMAN: Maybe it's a cultural thing. Whenever it's Shakespeare you have to give it a standing ovation.

MAN: No. I did *A Midsummer Night's Dream* once and no one got up at the end.

WOMAN: Maybe there's something we didn't understand.

Pause.

MAN: It's like people here are used to seeing crappy shows. There's no exploration of form.

WOMAN: That's not true. We saw some documentary theatre, that's exploration of form.

MAN: Yeah . . . that was interesting. But this . . . This was

just really shitty. We should've
left at intermission.

WOMAN: I thought we were
there to see your friend in
the show.

MAN: She's not my friend.
She's just a girl I met at that
audition.

WOMAN: It could've been a
good contact for you.

MAN: For what that's worth.

WOMAN: We should've gone to
talk to her instead of taking off
right after.

MAN: I wouldn't have known
what to say. It was soooo bad.

WOMAN: You could've lied.
You used to do it all the time
for your friends in Montréal.

*Pause. The MAN shoots her an
angry look.*

It's just that she looked like she
was nice. We could've gone for
a drink or something.

MAN: Nothing ever comes of it . . .

The WOMAN withdraws into herself, disappointed. A long pause.

Do you want me to text her? Maybe it's not too late.

WOMAN: No, it's fine. I just didn't think it would be this hard. I mean, we didn't move halfway across the earth. Just to a different city.

MAN: I know. And I bet there's people out there who are just as lonely as we are.

They look out for a moment at the audience.

AIR CANADA

*GILLES puts on a record. The
song "Lindbergh" by Robert
Charlebois plays.*

*The following information is
projected on the screen:*

> *From: YVR (Vancouver, BC)*
> *To: YUL (Montréal, QC)*
> *Departure: Dec. 23, 2012*
> *Return: Jan. 2, 2013*
> *Two Adults*
> *Total cost: $1826*
> *Funds available: $732*

*GILLES cuts out the music with
a scratch.*

NEW YEAR'S EVE

December 31, 2012

The MAN and WOMAN are sitting on the couch, wearing party hats. They are watching the video recorded at the beginning of the show of the crowd doing the countdown. They relive this moment with nostalgia.

The video ends and suddenly their apartment feels cold and bare.

WOMAN: Happy New Year.

MAN: Happy New Year, Esther.

They pull off their party hats and stare at the screen, both of them lost in their own thoughts.

PIECES OF YUL

GILLES: That spring, we went back to Montréal for a month. When we got there we started noticing things we hadn't before, like the construction everywhere, the buses that were always late, the smog, the politics going around in circles. It felt like the city fell to ruin during our absence.

But what had changed the most was the relationship to our friends and family. Their lives had carried on without us.

They project pictures of their friends.

ESTHER: This is Catherine. Before, we'd go see shows together every week. But she had moved to Brussels for an internship.

GILLES: My best friend Philippe. He'd just finished his master's in theatre, and I had just missed his graduating performance.

ESTHER: My friend Roxanne. She'd just bought a house in the suburbs. We tried to see each other, but it just didn't work out.

GILLES: My brother Jacques had sublet his place for the summer, so we barely saw each other.

ESTHER: When I visited my sister, my nephew didn't remember me.

GILLES: When we flew back at the end of the month, we found ourselves looking forward to Vancouver's laid-back vibe, its great public services, its fresh air, and its breathtaking scenery.

In fact, we weren't quite sure
if we were coming home or
leaving it, suspended in the
air between Montréal and
Vancouver.

WITHOUT YOU

*The WOMAN is doing some ori-
gami. The MAN is sitting in front
of his computer.*

MAN: Hey! It looks like I was
selected for that master class
in Ottawa.

WOMAN: *(coldly)* Oh, cool.

MAN: I think I'll go.

WOMAN: *(freezing)* Okay.

Pause.

MAN: What is it?

WOMAN: Nothing.

MAN: You're mad.

WOMAN: No. It's just that
you're always away, and when
you're not here, it's . . .

MAN: *(full on passive aggres-
sive)* I can cancel if you want.

WOMAN: Do what you want, Gilles.

MAN: I can tell it's bothering you.

Long pause.

WOMAN: It doesn't matter anyway.

MAN: What do you mean?

Long tense pause.

Esther, what do you mean?!

WOMAN: You want to know if it bothers me, but you'll end up going anyway.

MAN: It's a good opportunity to meet new people and network...

WOMAN: *(lashing out)* Well, I find it ironic that you're going to another city to make contacts when you don't even bother to do that here.

MAN: *(retorting)* I've tried, but you know how it is here.

People smile and shake your hand, and as soon as you turn your back they've forgotten your name. Anyhow, what's the use if we're going to move back to Montréal in six months.

Long pause.

WOMAN: I don't think I want to go back.

Pause.

Craig wants to extend my contract for another year, and I think I'll accept.

MAN: Okay.

Pause.

And if I want to move back, what do we do?

Pause. She says nothing.

Do I go without you?

Long pause.

WOMAN: I don't know . . .

TIME FLIES

GILLES: Our conversations
were sounding more and
more like that.

(to ESTHER) I don't know if
we'd still be together if it
weren't for your passport.

ESTHER: We were going on
vacation to France. When we
got to the airport the check-in
agent looked at my passport
and told me I couldn't leave
because it was expired.

GILLES: It was Friday, five
o'clock, and the passport
offices were closing.

(to ESTHER) I told you I wasn't
going to leave without you.

ESTHER: *(to GILLES)* I insisted
you catch your flight. I told
you I would join you as soon
as I could.

GILLES: We were standing in the middle of the airport. I was trying to reach Passport Canada one last time. You started to cry.

ESTHER: You went through security. You called me before getting on the plane, and then you were the one crying.

GILLES: I couldn't sleep the whole flight.

ESTHER: I went back to the apartment alone that night. When I met up with you in Paris, twenty-four hours later, something had changed between us: without saying a word, we had made a pact.

They smile at each other.

GILLES: *(to audience)* While we were on vacation, our landlords found out that we had rented out our place on Airbnb.

ESTHER: It wasn't allowed.

GILLES: So they kicked us out.

PART 3

13TH AVENUE EAST, VANCOUVER

PICK UP

September 1, 2013
13th Avenue East, Vancouver

*The MAN and WOMAN move into a
bigger apartment.*

MAN: This place is okay, right?

WOMAN: Don't you find it a bit
dark in here?

MAN: Yeah, no, it's because it's
cloudy out.

*Pause. They look around the
apartment.*

MAN: I know what's missing.
Come on.

*They leave the stage and make
their way to the table next to the
stage where GILLES is standing.*

MAN: How much for the
record player?

GILLES: A hundred bucks.

How about eighty?

Sure. Let's do eighty. Let me put it in a bag for you.

We're not going very far.

You sure? Looks like it might rain.

It's fine. We're not going very far.

GILLES unplugs the turntable and hands it over to the MAN.

WOMAN: He kind of looks like you.

MAN: What? No, he's way taller.

A crack of thunder, then rain.

ESTHER: That winter, it rained from November right through to May.

The MAN and WOMAN return to their apartment completely soaked.

The WOMAN grabs a towel and dries off her face. She then dries off the MAN's hair. They casually undress. The MAN returns with pyjamas. The WOMAN steals the pyjama top and slips it on. He slips on the bottoms.

LOVE TANK

The WOMAN *sits down comfort-*
ably on the couch with a book
while the MAN *puts on a record.*
He grabs another book and
joins her.

The turntable turns night
and day.
We lie there and we listen.
Like a lone radar
With one single ear for all.
—R. Ducharme

They snuggle, change positions,
and intertwine. Love, reading,
and sex.

At the end of the song, the MAN
and WOMAN *are stock-still,*
locked in each other's arms.

NOW WHAT

November 26, 2013

The couple is sitting on the couch, each holding a glass of wine.

MAN: What do you want to do tomorrow?

WOMAN: We could go to the farmers' market.

MAN: Nah, the Chinese grocery on Cambie is way cheaper.

WOMAN: We don't have to buy anything. We can just look at the vegetables.

MAN: I don't feel like looking at vegetables.

Pause.

WOMAN: Or we could go to Science World.

MAN: Yeah?! Where is that?

WOMAN: It's the big disco ball on Main Street.

MAN: Isn't that for kids?

WOMAN: Yeah . . .

MAN: Plus it's supposed to rain tomorrow.

WOMAN: Of course.

Pause.

MAN: Maybe we can stay on the couch and drink wine.

WOMAN: All day?

MAN: Sure.

WOMAN: We'll have to go out and buy more.

Pause.

MAN: Maybe I can make some.

WOMAN: What, wine?

MAN: Yeah.

WOMAN: Right, and I'll start making my own soap.

MAN: Taking baths and drinking wine. What more do you want?

WOMAN: And we're going to live off of what? Your royalties?!

MAN: Haha.

Pause.

I know, we'll sell your soap on the Internet.

WOMAN: Yeah! And we can grow some vegetables in the bath and get a chicken. We'll be self-sufficient and we'll never have to leave the apartment.

MAN: Maybe we can declare independence.

WOMAN: Our own country!?

MAN: More of a principality, like Monaco.

WOMAN: I could be the princess.

MAN: Okay. And our furniture can be our subjects.

Pause.

(turning to the furniture) No, Alexandre! Off with his head.

WOMAN: Hahaha. Maybe we pass a law making mime the official language.

MAN: Right, you're so good at it.

WOMAN: Refusal to mime is punishable by one year of imprisonment.

MAN: We'd have a prison?

They look around their small apartment.

WOMAN: . . . No.

She thinks.

We could deport them!

MAN: Where?

WOMAN: To the hallway.

MAN: Perfect. Next time the landlord comes for the rent, we deport him.

They laugh but can't seem to keep the game going. Boredom sets in. Time passes.

LIKE CHILDREN

February 30, 2014

WOMAN: What do we do now?

MAN: Maybe we can see who can stay on the couch the longest.

WOMAN: Okay!

MAN: Go?

WOMAN: Go.

They stay completely still.

MAN: How about we do something else at the same time.

WOMAN: Okay. How about from now on we only use the vowel "U"?

The MAN sits on the armrest. The WOMAN does the same.

74

MAN: Hullu.

WOMAN: Hullu. Huw uru yuu?

Pause. The WOMAN *tries another sentence.*

The wuuthur us bud tuduy. Su much ruun.

MAN: Whut?

WOMAN: Ut is ruunung.

The WOMAN *mimes rain falling from the sky.*

MAN: Uh, yus! Ut wus ruunung yusturduy. It ruun tuday. Ut wull ruun tumurruw. Ruuns ull thu tume.

WOMAN: Ruun. Ruun. Ruun.

Pause.

Uhm ... U'm u but hungru. Uru yuu hungru?

MAN: Yus. U'm vuru hungru. But thu rufrudgurutur us umptu. Wu huv nuthung tu uut.

75

WOMAN: Wu cuuld urdur fuud.

MAN: Whut?

WOMAN: Urdur!

The WOMAN mimes a phone receiver with her hand...

MAN: Yus! Urdur!

WOMAN: Whut du yuu wunt tu uut?

MAN: Hmm ... Puzzu.

The MAN mimes a pizza.

WOMAN: Yus. Puzzu!

MAN:. Puzzu wuth puppurunu, puppurs, mushruums.

WOMAN: No mushruums.

MAN:. Ul rught. Nu mushruums.

WOMAN: Und sume wune to drunk.

MAN: Rud wune or whute wune?

WOMAN: Uhm . . . rud wune. U would wunt u Utulun wune, muybu u sungiuvusu ur u chiuntu.

MAN: Huh?

WOMAN: U suud, u rud wune frum Utulu, u sungiuvusu ur u chiuntu.

MAN:. Sluw duwn. U dun't undurstund.

WOMAN: Lustun tu mu. U suud, u rud wune frum Utulu, u sungiuvusu ur u chiuntu.

MAN:. Whut?!

WOMAN: SUNGIUVUSU! CHIUNTU! RUD WUNE!

The MAN gives up.

MAN: This is boring, let's do something else.

The WOMAN looks around and spots the dictionary.

WOMAN: I know, let's play dictionary. I want to know every

English word in here by the time we leave this couch.

MAN: Okay.

The WOMAN cracks open the dictionary.

WOMAN: Okay... "A bone in the human leg, extending from the pelvis to the knee, that is the longest, largest, and strongest in the body."

MAN: Thigh bone.

WOMAN: Almost.

MAN: ... Femur.

WOMAN: Yes! Good.

MAN: Okay, ready? "A strong garment with long sleeves for confining the arms of a violent prisoner, mental patient, etc."

WOMAN: Wait, I know this...

She thinks hard.

The French word is "camisole de force!"

MAN: Yes. In English?

WOMAN: I don't know. Forced shirt?

MAN: Straightjacket.

WOMAN: How do you expect me to know that?

MAN: Everyone knows that.

WOMAN: Not me.

MAN: Well now you know.

WOMAN: My turn. "A very great or indefinitely great number of persons or things."

MAN: A lot? . . .
Many? . . .

WOMAN: Second definition: "Ten thousand."

MAN: Um . . . ten thousand? . . .
Huge? . . . I don't know. What is it?

WOMAN: Myriad.

MAN: What? Okay, that's super hard.

WOMAN: Well, now you know.

MAN: Haha. Okay. "A place where someone or something naturally belongs."

WOMAN: A habitat?

MAN: No.

WOMAN: A house?

MAN: Almost.

WOMAN: I don't know. Naturally belongs? Ah! A family?

MAN: No.

WOMAN: Well, what is it?

MAN: Home.

WOMAN: I said "house."

MAN: It's not the same thing. "House" is the physical structure, but "home" is ... Well ... I don't know how to translate

it. That word doesn't really
exist in French.

*A heavy feeling of solitude has
crept up on them.*

*The WOMAN seems affected by a
deep melancholy. The MAN looks
at her a moment, saddened to
see her like this. He picks up*
L'hiver de force *and starts
to read.*

Listen: "In a few months, we
will spend our time looking
at the tips of our shoes without being bored at all, with
the satisfaction of not having
to fight against this fierce
anguish. We'll be gone forever
but still here to revel in our
absence . . . "

WOMAN: What's that?

MAN: Réjean Ducharme.

Pause.

WOMAN: What else does
Réjean have to say?

MAN: "We didn't go out. We don't need to. We have all we need right here: coffee, milk, sugar, and the Greek on Marianne Street who lets us run a tab. [...] If people knew how easy life is when you're happy, they'd be happy all the time."

The MAN stops reading while the WOMAN ponders the passage. As the MAN returns to reading his book, the WOMAN springs up and heads to the dictionary.

You lost.

WOMAN: I'm not playing anymore.

She takes the dictionary and throws it out the window.

MAN: Hey ... What are you doing?

WOMAN: We don't need it anymore. It's like he says: we have all we need right here—coffee, milk, sugar ...

MAN: ...

WOMAN: We don't need anything else.

MAN: You're right. Fuck it.

He jumps up and throws Réjean Ducharme's book out the window.

No matter how many times I read it, it never ends well.

They smile at each other.

Okay. So what do we call our principality?

WOMAN: Maybe we don't give it a name: that way no one can find us.

PERMANENT VACATION

The MAN and WOMAN look around their newly created principality. The WOMAN rushes to the table, grabs a pair of scissors, and starts to cut out a piece of paper. She unfolds the paper: it forms a paper crown. She puts it on the MAN's head. She picks up the throw from the couch and drapes herself in it. Side by side, prince and princess, they ceremoniously wave at their furniture subjects.

A nervous smile flashes across the WOMAN's face as she looks at the MAN. He rushes over to the turntable and puts on a record. He grabs her by the hand and they start to dance. They dance all over the apartment; they dance to exhaustion. The WOMAN drops on the couch, and the MAN tugs on her hand, trying to get her up to keep the party going. He finally abandons her and keeps dancing solo around the couch.

Janbruary 34, 2U1?

*Slowly the air in the apartment
changes: the MAN continues to
dance frenetically around the
room. The WOMAN grabs her
scissors and paper and begins to
make cut-out trees. She realizes
that she can't seem to remember
how to do a proper cut-out.
An intense anguish takes hold
of her.*

*The MAN is now pacing frantically around the apartment. He
moves like a tiger in a cage, as if
something boils in the pit of his
stomach. He wanders around
the space aimlessly, searching
for something to take his mind
off this growing feeling of angst.
He stumbles on a pile of books
and starts to flip through them
urgently, looking for something
he cannot find.*

*The WOMAN is clutching her
head. Everything has become
too overwhelming. She wraps
herself completely into the
throw blanket like a human-
sized cocoon.*

The MAN makes his way behind the couch and starts going through the boxes. He dumps the contents out and a cascade of books rains down on the floor.

The WOMAN abandons the throw blanket. She breathes heavily as she looks about tensely, trying to find a way to shut out the outside world. She picks up one of the cardboard boxes and throws its contents on the floor. She covers her head with it as if the box's darkness will provide her shelter from her growing panic.

The MAN begins to throw the books all over the apartment as he continues his search.

The WOMAN now sees a roll of toilet paper on the floor. She begins to wrap it around her head in an attempt to block out the noise and light. Her head is now completely mummified, but it is still not enough to block out the outside world. She grasps at whatever object she finds on the floor and grabs hold of a few party hats. She sets the party hats over her eyes, ears,

and hands. She now looks like a
strange insect, completely still.

The MAN has taped some of
the books together and has
attached them to his body like
a belt. It makes him look like
a suicide bomber. He rips up
any loose pages he can find and
pretends to blow himself up,
throwing bits of literary confetti
about the room.

The MAN paces behind the couch
and is getting more and more
tense. As he walks up to the
front of the couch, he catches
sight of the WOMAN. His heart
sinks—what has happened
to them. He walks towards
the woman with contained
anger. He turns to the couch
and unleashes his fury onto it,
yelling and punching it before
flipping it over in an excess
of rage. Hearing his screams,
the WOMAN tears the paper and
party hats from her head. She
gently approaches him and
touches his shoulder to see if
he's okay. The MAN is startled
by her touch and jumps like a
wounded animal.

STRANGE LOVE

*Visibly shaken, they look into
each other's eyes. The MAN
takes off the last party hat
from the WOMAN's head: she
gently arranges his dishev-
elled hair. They look at each
other intensely. The WOMAN
notices that the MAN is no longer
wearing his crown. She looks
around and picks up a plastic
bag from the floor. She del-
icately places it on his head
as a replacement. She slowly
pulls the bag down on his head,
like an astronaut helmet. The
MAN smiles and opens the bag,
inviting the WOMAN in. She
slips her head into the bag and
they kiss as if melding into
each other, squeezing the bag
around their heads. The plastic
bag expands and retracts with
each breath. As their embrace
gets more intense, they fall to
the ground. Their breathing
accelerates as they search for*

air. After a moment that seems like an eternity, the WOMAN *rips the bag off their heads, gasping for air. They seem stunned by what they've just done. The* MAN *catches his breath. He glances at the* WOMAN, *checking to see if she's all right. He slowly rises and walks over to her and helps her up. He wraps his arms around her and they hold each other. They slowly notice the state of their surroundings. As if emerging from a dream they look around at their trashed apartment.*

THE CITY

*The MAN and WOMAN slowly
gather their clothes off the
ground in an effort to clean up
their apartment. GILLES and
ESTHER join them on stage to
help. They all start placing the
different items in a very orga-
nized fashion in the middle of
the stage. Boxes, books, a towel,
a wine bottle, and glasses all
come together to form a strange
city on stage.*

*Chalk is pulled out and street
names are drawn on the apartment floor.*

*The city contains Chemin
Duquette, with a house and
forest; Rue Dorion with the
Montréal condo; the beach and
the sea; mountains; Bo-Bec
Ice Cream on Laurier Avenue;
the Burrard Street Bridge; the
Eiffel Tower with Mark and
Anita; Science World; and
Cambie Street.*

After a moment, the MAN *and* WOMAN *look at* GILLES *and* ESTHER *and exit the apartment, leaving them alone.*

ESTHER: It was a night at the end of winter: we couldn't sleep so we went outside for a walk. We walked for a long time in the empty streets. Vancouver was beautiful. We felt like we had the city all to ourselves. And maybe it was just because of the warm morning light, but it seemed to us that spring had sprung overnight. The rain had stopped and the cherry trees had bloomed into big bouquets of cotton candy. The city streets began to fill up, and for the first time we felt that we were part of it all. We didn't quite know how, but it seemed that we had finally found our way back home.

Noir.

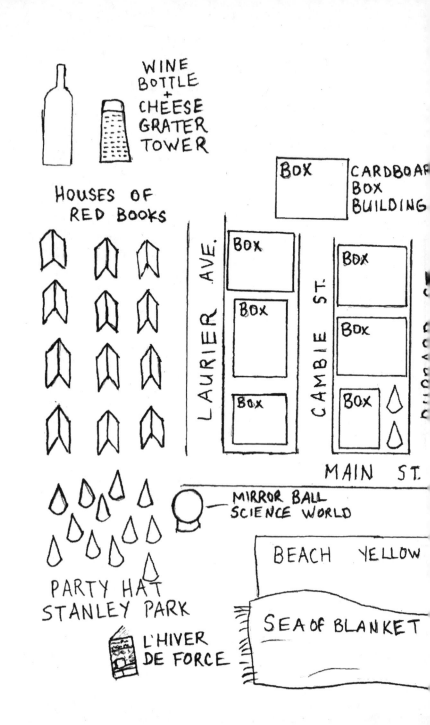

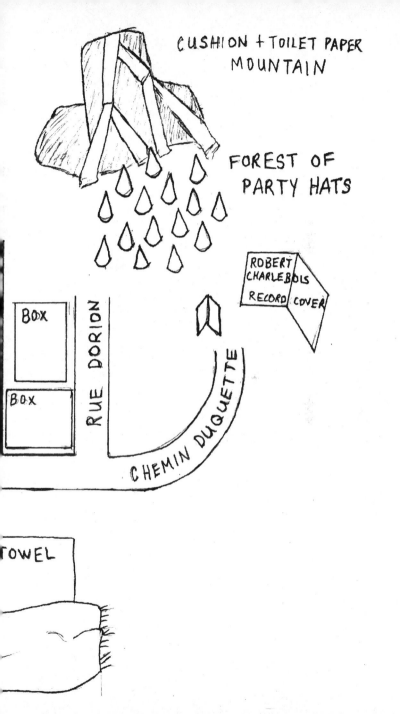

CUSHION + TOILET PAPER
MOUNTAIN

FOREST OF
PARTY HATS

ROBERT
CHARLEBOIS
RECORD COVER

BOX

RUE DORION

CHEMIN DUQUETTE

BOX

TOWEL

ACKNOWLEDGEMENTS

We would like to thank the following organizations for their support: l'Association des théâtres francophones du Canada, Carrefour international de théâtre de Québec, the Playwrights Theatre Centre, the Only Animal, the Banff Centre for Arts and Creativity, the National Theatre School of Canada, la Fondation pour l'avancement du théâtre francophone au Canada, the Canada Council for the Arts, and the BC Arts Council. We would also like to thank Anne-Marie Guilmaine and Mélanie Dumont for their advice, Ludger Beaulieu, Joëlle Bond, Mark Chavez, Maxime Robin, Anita Rochon, and David Trottier for their collaboration during the creative process. And a very special thanks to Cory Haas, who helped us create this piece by participating as an actor in numerous development phases. Last but not least, we would like to express our deepest thanks to Frédéric Lemay and Julie Trépanier for their generosity, patience, and most of all talent. It was an immense pleasure to share the stage with you.

 Esther Duquette has been the artistic director of Théâtre la Seizième since 2016. A graduate of the Université du Québec à Montréal in journalism with a specialization in theatre and literature, she centres her practice on artistic counselling, directing, and dramaturgy. Her first play, *Straight Jacket Winter*, was presented across Canada from 2016 to 2019. The recipient of the Prix Roland Mahé-Banque Nationale, Esther has also received three Jessie Richardson Theatre Award nominations for her work. She co-founded the Vancouver-based company 2PAR4 in 2015, and has sat on the boards of a number of artistic companies and associations since 2012. She currently lives in Vancouver.

Originally from Saskatoon, Saskatchewan, Gilles Poulin-Denis is an actor, playwright, director, translator, and dramaturg. His first full-length play, *Rearview*, was presented in both French and English in Sudbury in 2016. It was later published by Dramaturges Éditeurs and was nominated for the 2010 Governor General's Literary Award. Wajdi Mouawad named Gilles as one of the resident playwrights at the National Arts Centre's French Theatre, where he developed his play *Dehors*. *Dehors* was published by L'Instant-Scène in 2017. Gilles has collaborated on numerous devised pieces, such as *ishow, Après la Peur*, and *Gabriel Dumont's Wild West Show*. Gilles is the artistic director of 2PAR4 and currently lives in Vancouver.

First edition: November 2019
Printed and bound in Canada by Rapido Books, Montréal

Jacket photo by Emily Cooper Photography
Jacket design based on the work of Atelier Mille Mille
Author photos © Julie Artacho

 **PLAYWRIGHTS
CANADA PRESS**
202-269 Richmond St. W.
Toronto, ON
M5V 1X1

416.703.0013
info@playwrightscanada.com
www.playwrightscanada.com
@playcanpress